MOVIE · POSTER · BOOK

Stars of the Fifties

MARK LEWIS

OCTOPUS BOOKS

ACKNOWLEDGEMENTS

The publishers thank the following for providing the photographs in this book:
Aquarius Literary Agency, Joel Finler, Ronald Grant Archive, The Kobal Collection, The Naphthine-Walsh
Collection, The National Film Archive.

First published in 1986 by Octopus Books Limited
59 Grosvenor Street, London W1

© 1986 Octopus Books Limited

ISBN 0 7064 2637 3

First impression

Printed in Hong Kong

CONTENTS

INTRODUCTION

The sensation of 1940 was Carmen Miranda. Ten years later it was Marlon Brando, an indication of the sea change which the star system had undergone in the intervening years.

During the war cinemagoing had reached a peak. Virtually anything on celluloid was guaranteed an audience, and in the firmament the great fixed stars – Clark Gable, Bette Davis, Robert Taylor, Joan Crawford – shone brightly. But by the end of the decade the empires on which their fortunes had been built were fast crumbling. The major studios were forced to split their theatre organisations from the production-distribution side of their business. The McCarthy witch hunt had spread its tentacles into the film capital, setting in motion a debilitating cycle of fear and betrayal. Costs were spiralling, fresh ideas were nowhere to be found, and on the horizon a new and increasingly powerful competitor – television – rode into view. With its steady diet of domestic comedies, cop thrillers and Westerns, television quickly killed off the ailing B-movie industry, for so long the forcing ground for new talent and the pasture on which fading stars were put out to graze.

In the early 1950s Universal was the only studio to maintain an old-fashioned 'slave market' of young talent, and the investment paid off in the persons of Tony Curtis and Rock Hudson, who served their apprenticeships in the last spate of Hollywood adventure movies. Now television could provide the first rung on the ladder and, significantly, Charlton Heston and Grace Kelly were both spotted on the small screen. They made their way in Hollywood where anxiety about the future was combined with a nostalgic rummaging around in the past – when Kelly became a star all MGM could dream up for her was a succession of lavish remakes of past hits. Cut loose from their comfortable moorings, old-style stars like Robert Taylor drifted forlorn and rudderless. Others younger and more vigorous took advantage of the fragmenting studio system to set up their own production companies. Notable examples were Kirk Douglas and Burt Lancaster, while James Stewart signed an innovatory contract with Universal whereby he took a percentage of his films' profits. Fighting a rearguard action against television, the studios experimented with big screens, 3-D, and even Richard Egan as 'the new Clark Gable'. But cinema audiences were now far more interested in the sexual candour of continental sensations like Brigitte Bardot. What irked the moguls most was the feeling of control slipping through their fingers. The explosive arrival and equally swift departure of a James Dean was something no studio could anticipate, while Monroe became a star virtually in spite of 20th Century-Fox's attempts to mould her into a dumb blonde sex bomb.

In 1951 Hollywood had produced over 400 movies. By 1959 the figure was down to 171. However, in the final analysis it is the image on the screen which counts, and the decade produced many which were as memorable as those in the heyday of the dream factory. Above all, it was the magic presence of the stars which gave shape and substance to the dreams and, in these pages, we hope to re-awaken some of the cherished memories.

DORIS DAY

DORIS DAY

Real name **Doris von Kappelhoff**
Born **Cincinnati, Ohio, 3 April 1924**

Doris Day has the apparent simplicity of a Pop Art painting. Cheerful, chaste, eternally optimistic, her name summons images of automobile ads of the early 50s, in which guys in white tuxedos escorted busty, fresh-faced blondes towards a Cadillac and a Technicolor sunset.

In contrast, Doris Day's early career was a struggle. As a teenager she survived a near-fatal car crash and two disastrous marriages, fighting her way up from local radio stations to singing with Bob Crosby's band. A spot on the nationally networked 'Saturday Night Hit Parade' led to an audition with Warner director Michael Curtiz. She cried with nervousness all the way through, but made her debut soon afterwards, replacing a pregnant Betty Hutton in *Romance On the High Seas* (1948), and singing 'It's Magic' which became a solid hit. She moved on to straight parts in *Young Man With A Horn* (1950) about trumpeter Bix Beiderbecke, in which she played Kirk Douglas' put-upon girlfriend, and *Storm Warning* (1950), in which she was murdered by the Ku Klux Klan. But it was in a series of unpretentious, undemanding musicals – *The West Point Story* (1950), *Lullaby Of Broadway* (1951), *I'll See You In My Dreams* (1951), *April In Paris* (1952) – that she became a top box-office star, showing herself to be as accomplished an actress as she was a singer.

Her records sold in millions and young girls worked hard at imitating her fluffy, wholesome style. She hit a more strident note in *Calamity Jane* (1953) – trying to outdo the gusto of Betty Hutton's *Annie Get Your Gun* (1950) – and then attempted to broaden her range in the biopic *Love Me Or Leave Me* (1955), piling on the agony as torch singer Ruth Etting who suffered under the possessive protection of a psychopathic gangster (James Cagney). In Hitchcock's *The Man Who Knew Too Much* (1956), teamed with James Stewart, she rather tiresomely and repeatedly sang 'Que Sera, Sera', but was otherwise sympathetic as a mother whose small son is kidnapped. She was at her perky best in *The Pajama Game* (1956) a snappy version of a Broadway hit, and then slipped into a long run of romantic comedies: *Tunnel Of Love* (1958), *Teacher's Pet* (1958) and *Pillow Talk* (1959), the first of a number of smoothly crafted outings with Rock Hudson which substituted mildly salacious innuendo for sex. Nevertheless, it is a reflection of Day's energy and professionalism that she survived unscathed into the very different atmosphere of the 60s. She scored a big hit in *That Touch Of Mink* (1962) and bustled breezily through *Move Over Darling* (1963), but the endless jokes about 'Miss Chastity Belt' were beginning to catch up with her. Virtually every so-called Hollywood wit claimed to have known Doris Day 'before she was a virgin'. A disastrous return to the musical in Billy Rose's *Jumbo* (1963) – more of a turkey than a pachyderm – robbed her of *The Sound Of Music* and *The Unsinkable Molly Brown*, and since *The Glass-Bottomed Boat* (1966) she has regrettably done little of any interest.

Her partial retirement can to some extent be explained by the death, in 1968, of her third husband, Marty Melcher, and her subsequent discovery that in the management of her affairs he had been robbing her blind. She still looks as fresh as farmhouse butter but now seems content with appearing in margarine ads on the television.

with Thelma Ritter in *Pillow Talk*

TONY CURTIS

TONY CURTIS

*Real name **Bernard Schwartz***
*Born **Bronx, New York, 3 June 1925***

Hollywood has ever been the realm of improbability. In *Lloyds Of London* (1936), Freddie Bartholomew grows up to be Tyrone Power. In *The Wolf Man* (1941), hulking Lon Chaney Jr towers over his father, dapper little Claude Rains. In this context it is not the least surprising that Bernie Schwartz, the Jewish bad boy from the Bronx, should become *The Prince Who Was A Thief* (1951) and *The Son Of Ali Baba* (1952), possessor of a world-famous, much-imitated haircut and the recipient of 10,000 letters a week begging for a lopped-off curl.

After war service in the navy, drama school, and the lead in an off-Broadway production of 'Golden Boy', he was signed by Universal. The studio groomed him for stardom in the old-fashioned way, and a lengthy apprenticeship included bit parts in *City Across The River* (1948), as a young hoodlum, and *Johnny Stoolpigeon,* as a mute killer. By the time *Kansas Raiders* (1950) came around he was fifth on the cast list, and his popularity encouraged Universal to star him in a succession of cut-rate actioners and costume adventures. Among them was *The Black Shield Of Falworth* (1954) in which he delivered the immortal line 'Yonda lies da castle of my faddah', in purest Bronx. Nevertheless, he was athletic, looked good in tights, didn't take himself too seriously and could act, as he showed in the title role in *Houdini* (1953). He was still in tights for Burt Lancaster's circus drama *Trapeze* (1956), but it led to the part of the grovelling press agent Sidney Falco, opposite Lancaster's vicious gossip columnist J. J. Hunsecker in Alexander Mackendrick's *Sweet Smell Of Success* (1957). It marked a return to Curtis' urban roots and, as David

Thomson has observed, was a portrait of 'a man on all fours some years before America really noticed the posture'. In between more costume epics – *The Vikings* (1958), *Spartacus* (1960) and *Taras Bulba* (1962) – he reinforced his credentials as a dramatic actor in *The Defiant Ones* (1958), manacled to Sidney Poitier, and established himself as an accomplished comedian in *Some Like It Hot* (1959). Far more subtle and relaxed in drag than his companion Jack Lemmon, he stole the show with a wicked impersonation of his hero Cary Grant (a gag he has unwisely repeated in a number of films). After *Operation Petticoat* (1960), co-starring with Grant, he was *The Great Imposter* (1960), a performance which curiously reflected his own fragile grasp of himself. He was the tragic Indian war hero Ira Hayes in *The Outsider* (1961), but the film was mangled by the studio. He retreated into a dismal spiral of comedies before disappearing beneath a built-up nose as unlikely as any Universal armour to play Albert de Salvo, *The Boston Strangler* (1968).

No one seemed to know what to do with him in the 1970s. The worst of a string of disastrous films was Mae West's *Sextette* (1978), the most disappointing *Lepke* (1974) – a missed opportunity as the Jewish mobster running Murder Incorporated. He seemed happier slumming it on TV in 'Vegas' and toying with the audience on chat shows, but Nicolas Roeg hauled him back from the dead in *Insignificance* (1985), to give an oleaginously evil performance as Senator Joseph McCarthy. In the 50s, Tony Curtis was popularly married to actress Janet Leigh. They are the parents of the attractive and talented Jamie Lee Curtis.

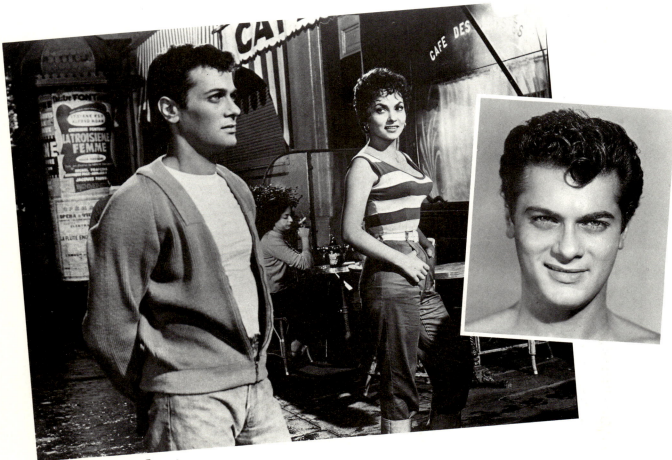

with Gina Lollobrigida in *Trapeze*

CHARLTON HESTON

CHARLTON HESTON

*Real name **Charles Carter***
*Born **Evanston, Illinois, 4 October 1923***

Charlton Heston's aquiline features, piercing blue eyes and majestic, tanned torso have always marked him out as a warrior hero. He looks uncomfortable in blazer and flannels but fills out a suit of chainmail in all the right places. This monolithic presence suggests limitations as an actor, and in some of his films there is an uneasy feeling that the longer he goes on talking the less interesting he becomes. Between massively dignified repose and slightly musclebound action there is often little room for Heston to provide his characters with an inner life beneath the nobly furrowed brow. Perhaps his most disarming quality is the determination to impress on his audience that underneath the guise of action star there beats the heart of a sensitive and articulate actor.

Heston has always had pretentions to playing the classics – eventually taking a stab at Antony in *Antony And Cleopatra* on film in 1972 – and he was spotted on television, playing Rochester in 'Jane Eyre', by Hal Wallis and cast as the callow World War II veteran turned gambler in *Dark City* (1950). But it was DeMille who set him on his way as the hardbitten circus owner in *The Greatest Show On Earth* (1952), only the actor's second film. A succession of rugged action roles followed: an Indian in *The Savage* (1952); Buffalo Bill in *Pony Express* (1953); and an Amazonian planter in *The Naked Jungle* (1954). These were little more than programmers, as were *Arrowhead* (1953) and *Lucy Gallant* but, in between, *Ruby Gentry* (1952) gave him the chance to swagger about as Jennifer Jones' lover, and in *The President's Lady* (1953) he played Andrew Jackson in such magisterial style that five years later Anthony Quinn asked him to repeat

the role in *The Buccaneer* (1958). Nevertheless, he might have gone to semi-oblivion had not DeMille ridden to the rescue with the monumental part of Moses in *The Ten Commandments* (1956). After *Three Violent People* (1957) his self-improving urge led him to take a supporting and self-effacing role in Orson Welles' *Touch of Evil* (1958). He was excellent in *The Big Country* (1958), directed by William Wyler who also steered him through his Oscar-winning performance in the title role of *Ben-Hur* (1959), the supreme test of his stamina and application. In Anthony Mann's *El-Cid* (1962) he effortlessly assumed the mantle of legend, while in *55 Days At Peking* (1963) Nicholas Ray persuaded him to be both reflective and fleetingly vulnerable in a scene with a small Chinese child. He then went on to outpoint Olivier in *Khartoum* (1966). At 45 he was still equal to the strenuous task of *Planet Of The Apes* (1968) before crossing the threshold of middle age in *Will Penny* (1968) as an illiterate cowboy, and *Number One* (1969) as a fading football star.

In the 70s he worked his way grimly into the 20th century via a series of disaster films, the decade's equivalent of the epic: *Earthquake* (1974), *Airport* (1974), *Grey Lady Down* (1978). He also played Cardinal Richelieu in *The Three Musketeers* (1974) and *The Four Musketeers* (1975). He has looked as virile as ever in more recent movies – *The Mountain Men* (1980) and *Mother Lode* (1982) – but ironically, just the kind of routine actioners with which he began his career. However, a critically acclaimed performance on the London stage as Captain Queeg in 'The Caine Mutiny' (1985) is an indication that he might allow himself to grow old gracefully.

in Ben-Hur

JAMES DEAN

JAMES DEAN

Born **Marion, Indiana, 8 February 1931**
Died **1955**

In the mid-50s cool young men tried hard to look just like James Dean. In the mid-1980s cool young men are trying just as hard. Dean was anything but cool. Director Elia Kazan called him 'a pudding of hatred', and candid photographs of the bespectacled, slightly pudgy young man hint at the tantrum-prone depressive skulking behind the iconic image of the *Rebel Without A Cause* (1955). In his brief time at the top he was compared with Brando. But Marlon is still with us, grown fat and bald while husbanding his fires. Perhaps Dean might have survived to become the man in *Last Tango In Paris* (1972). Or he might have grown twisted and bitter with age, like Jett Rink, the character he played in *Giant* (1955), threshing about in a rage of wasted energies. Death, perhaps, was the shrewdest of career moves, freezing Dean in the sullenly romantic image of the anti-hero, the lost leader of the beat generation.

While studying at UCLA he joined a drama group and secured bit parts in three movies – *Fixed Bayonets* (1951). *Sailor Beware* (1951) and *Has Anybody Seen My Gal?* (1952). On the urging of actor James Whitmore he joined the Actors' Studio in New York and for a while lived as a bisexual urban nomad. A much reproduced photograph immortalises Dean during this period, hunched in an overcoat several sizes too big, with pinched features and unruly hair, slouching through the puddles of a Big City rainstorm. He began to establish himself on television in 'mixed-up teenager' roles, before an award-winning performance as the blackmailing Arab boy in a Broadway version of Gide's 'The Immoralist' brought him to the attention of Elia Kazan, who cast him, opposite Julie Harris, as Cal

in Steinbeck's *East Of Eden* (1955). 'Picturegoer' readers voted him their Best Actor award and powerful newspaper columnist Hedda Hopper, who had seen them all come and helped not a few of them to go, raved 'I couldn't remember ever having seen a young man with such power . . . so much sheer invention'. In Nicholas Ray's *Rebel Without A Cause* (1955) he formed a touching trio with Sal Mineo and Natalie Wood (both of whom were also to meet tragic ends, the former brutally murdered and the latter drowned while swimming off a sailing boat). The film's title is a misnomer – he was not so much a rebel as a disillusioned romantic, a dreamer anticipating his generation's disenchantment with the bland, empty lines of American materialism. His last film, George Stevens' *Giant* (1955), is more coarse-grained, a sprawling family epic in which he was required to age – not wholly convincingly – from a young cowhand to a middle-aged oil tycoon. Dennis Hopper recalls that before Dean played his first scene with Elizabeth Taylor, he suddenly walked towards the big crowd of spectators and urinated in front of them. Asked why he had done it, he replied that if he could do that in front of so many people he could do anything with Taylor in front of the camera.

James Dean was born in Indiana in 1931. He was killed driving his Porsche just as *Giant* finished shooting, his death prompting an hysterical response which drew comparisons with that of Valentino, and the date of the tragedy, September 30, 1955 becoming the title of a film. He was just 24 years old when he departed this earth, leaving his legend behind for future young generations to worship.

with Elizabeth Taylor in Giant

KIM NOVAK

KIM NOVAK

Real name **Marilyn Pauline Novak**
Born **Chicago, Illinois, 13 February 1933**

She was discovered touring the States advertising refrigerators as 'Miss Deepfreeze'. She never quite thawed out under the studio lights, and the element of strain which clings to her work led critics to claim that she couldn't act. But the impassive eye of the camera oftens seeks out qualities more elusive than the flashy technique of 'great actresses'. The tension between Kim Novak's almost desperately solemn concentration and her shy blonde beauty propels her gently towards the centre of even the most mediocre films in which she appeared, and gives a haunting edge to a masterpiece like Hitchcock's *Vertigo* (1958), an extra dimension which was accepted without remark when the movie was made but is growing more resonant with the passage of time.

At Columbia, the studio's powerful star-making boss, Harry Cohn, built her up as a replacement for his now fading personal favourite Rita Hayworth. In contrast to some of the more synthetic of her contemporaries, she was natural and bashful, sometimes opting not to wear a bra in the heyday of the C-Cup, and blessed with the kind of Botticelli figure dreamed of by every small-town cocktail waitress who has ever fantasised about breaking into the movies. In *Pushover* (1954) she was a gangster's moll seducing cop Fred MacMurray. In *Phfft* (1954) – which is the sound of a marriage breaking up – she provided Jack Lemmon with some extra-marital activity but, still unsure of herself, seemed like a pale copy of Monroe. After *Five Against The House* (1955) the studio starred her in *Picnic* (1955), as the country girl stolen from Cliff Robertson by William Holden. By the time she was saving heroin addict Frank Sinatra from the needle by locking herself up with him in *The Man With The Golden Arm* (1955), the camera was beginning to coax out her beauty. She looked ravishing as Tyrone Power's wife in *The Eddie Duchin Story* (1956) and then, in another biopic played the doomed silent star *Jeanne Eagels* (1957). In *Pal Joey* (1957), again with Sinatra, she sang 'My Funny Valentine' with poignant gravity and did a gauche striptease. Then Richard Quine drew a touching performance from her in *Bell, Book And Candle* (1958), as a witch yearning to be human. In the same year she made *Vertigo*. Filming always seemed an ordeal for Novak, and never more so than in this rapt, almost trancelike performance. It is as if the normal barriers between actor and audience have been removed.

After *Strangers When We Meet* (1960) – again for Quine and co-starring Kirk Douglas – a tale of suburban infidelity in which she touched another wistful chord, her career fell sharply away. Her last good part was in Billy Wilder's *Kiss Me Stupid* (1964), as Polly the Pistol, a waitress-cum-whore hired to masquerade as a respectable housewife and tickle Dean Martin's jaded palate. In her new found domesticity, she forgets the routine seduction. She was cast as an old-style movie queen in Robert Aldrich's *The Legend of Lylah Clare* (1968), an approximation of her own position. Sadly, the film disappeared without trace. She is much heavier now and, apart from *The White Buffalo* (1977) and *Just A Gigolo* (1979), which boasted Marlene Dietrich and David Bowie in the cast, but to little avail, Novak has been little seen of late. But *Vertigo* remains to ensure her a lasting place in the memory.

with Fred MacMurray in *Pushover*

ROCK HUDSON

ROCK HUDSON

Real name **Roy Scherer**
Born **Winnetka, Illinois, 17 November 1925**
Died **1985**

In 1954 husky young Roy was a Navy laundryman, third class. Four years later Universal Studios renamed him 'Rock', hid his shirt and set about manufacturing him into a movie star in the old-fashioned way. First came bit parts in programmers like *I Was A Shoplifter* (1950), and then bigger roles in cut-rate actioners and costume adventures: *Tomahawk* (1951), *Iron Man* (1951), and *Scarlet Angel* (1952), starring Yvonne de Carlo. He wasn't very good – about as animated as a cigar store Indian – and years later he recalled that most of his early films 'make me cringe – it's like having your dirty linen washed in public'. But he was sincere, hard-working and eager to learn, qualities which sustained him while other beefcake contemporaries slipped into obscurity.

After an unbroken run of actioners – *Sea Devils* (1953), *The Golden Blade* (1953), *Taza Son Of Cochise* (1954) – there came a change of direction. In *Magnificent Obsession* (1955), Douglas Sirk uncovered the innately gentle and sympathetic character concealed beneath the muscular exterior. Hudson played the drunken playboy who redeems himself after accidentally blinding Jane Wyman, and his softly romantic glare and aura of quiet authority made him an ideal sustaining figure in melodrama: *All That Heaven Allows* (1955), *Never Say Goodbye* (1956), *Written On the Wind* (1957), and *The Tarnished Angels* (1957) in which his performance as an alcoholic reporter hinted at depths he was later either unable or unwilling to explore. Growing in confidence and box-office popularity, he turned in workmanlike performances in *Giant* (1956), *Something Of Value* (1957), the remake of *A Farewell To Arms* (1959)

with Jennifer Jones, and *This Earth Is Mine* (1959). Then he turned his attention to comedy in *Pillow Talk* (1959), sharing a party line with Doris Day. Amiably flustered or calculatedly philandering, Hudson partnered Day in two more plush, undemanding comedies, *Lover Come Back* (1962) and *Send Me No Flowers* (1964). One critic likened them to two shiny new Cadillacs parked side by side. He was less happily paired with Gina Lollobrigida in *Come September* (1961), but endearing opposite Paula Prentiss in *Man's Favourite Sport* (1964) as the self-styled angling authority who has never caught a fish. In between the comedies there were a number of offbeat failures: *The Last Sunset* (1961), *The Spiral Road* (1962) and *A Gathering Of Eagles* (1963).

His career wound down after *Seconds* (1966), a science fiction thriller in which John Frankenheimer cleverly exploited his lack of a clearly defined screen personality by casting him as an elderly businessman rebuilt by plastic surgery into his own image. After *Pretty Maids All In A Row* (1971) the tide went out, leaving Hudson beached in an anodyne TV series, *McMillan And Wife*. In the early 80s he was clearly ailing, the poor health paring down his good looks to reveal a more gaunt and interesting face. Alas, what was not known until shortly before his death in 1985 was that the increasingly haggard star was tragically a victim of AIDS. Many of his Hollywood friends and colleagues, with Elizabeth Taylor at the vanguard, have held functions to raise funds for research into the disease, and to campaign for a better understanding of it. Rock Hudson was held in true affection by the movie colony.

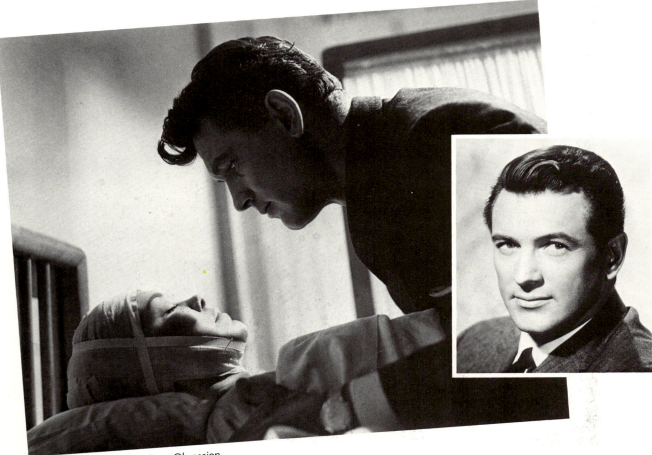

with Jane Wyman in Magnificent Obsession

MARILYN MONROE

MARILYN MONROE

Real name **Norma Jean Baker**
Born **Los Angeles, California, 1 June 1926**
Died **1962**

More words have been spilled over Monroe than any other postwar star. Biographies and memoirs strive to arrange into a recognisable mosaic the shards of a dislocated and disordered life. Ultimately, the magic defies analysis. Like her 20s predecessor Clara Bow, Monroe simply had 'It', that mysterious instinctive quality which makes the screen glow. Also like Bow, she had a frightful childhood – filled with fantasies of Clark Gable as a father – and married her first husband at 16 simply to forestall a spell in the county orphanage. After the war she drifted into model work and then, like a thousand other blonde hopefuls, the movies. In her first three films she made little impact, but then she was ogled by Groucho Marx in *Love Happy* (1949), and had her jaw remodelled and nose bob-tipped at the suggestion of her mentor, the agent Johnny Hyde.

Most of her early films reveal a forlorn starlet unsure of what to do with so luscious a body, but there were flashes of what was to come. In *The Asphalt Jungle* (1950) she merely had to sprawl across a sofa in Louis Calhern's penthouse to charge the scene with sexual static; in *All About Eve* (1950) she appeared briefly on George Sanders' arm, drawlingly introduced as a 'graduate of the Copacabana School of Dramatic Art'. The joke is meant to be on her, but the image lingers. By now 20th Century-Fox had marked her down for bigger things, launching a barrage of shameless publicity gimmicks, including the famous nude photographs. By the time she made *Clash By Night* (1952), nominally starring Barbara Stanwyck, journalists were swarming over the set to photograph 'the broad with the big tits'. Fox pushed the image hard: she was the dumb but knowing

secretary in *Monkey Business* (1952) – 'half child, but not the half that shows', as Cary Grant observes; poured into a skintight red sheath in *Niagara* (1953); a gold digger in *Gentlemen Prefer Blondes* (1953) and *How To Marry A Millionaire* (1954); and a hatcheck girl aching to play Chekhov – an ironic anticipation of her own aspirations at The Actors' Studio – in *There's No Business Like Show Business* (1954). She was still tentative, but had acquired her immortal wide-eyed, open-mouthed look, captured so famously by Andy Warhol in his pop painting.

She was also increasingly ruled by the instability to which she had long been prone. It wrecked her brief marriage to baseballer Joe DiMaggio, surrounded her with a nagging entourage of advisers and coaches and propelled her into the arms of Arthur Miller in a quest for intellectual respectability. In *The Seven-Year Itch* (1955) director Billy Wilder and co-star Tom Ewell seemed to leer at her sexuality, but in *Bus Stop* (1956) she came closest to a fully realised character as the floozie who drives cowboy Don Murray wild. *Some Like It Hot* (1959) was made when she was rushing towards breakdown, but in spite of the tantrums, walk-outs and forgotten lines she delivered a richly comic performance. In *The Misfits* (1961) she made her melancholy, long deferred rendezvous with Clark Gable. Crack-up lay around the corner. Deserted by her lovers, the last of whom was Bobby Kennedy, and awash with pills, she died from an overdose on 5 August 1962. Fragments from the uncompleted *Something's Got To Give*, particularly a nude swimming scene, show that she was still luminously beautiful. The camera loved her to the end.

with Elliott Reid in Gentlemen Prefer Blondes

MARLON BRANDO

MARLON BRANDO

*Born **Omaha, Nebraska, 3 April 1924***

As Jack Nicholson observed while they were making *The Missouri Breaks* (1976), 'He's still the one to beat'. While Marlon Brando may seem at times like a man bemused by, rather than in control of, his superabundant talent, he continues to command respect, attention, and colossal salaries. He was educated at Shattuck Military Academy – from which he was expelled – and studied drama at the Actors' Studio, remaining its most famous pupil. In 1946 he was voted Broadway's Most Promising Actor and in the following year scored an immense success as the brutish Stanley Kowalski – a kind of Caliban with sex appeal – in Tennessee Williams' 'A Streetcar Named Desire'.

Hollywood could wait no longer and Stanley Kramer signed him for *The Men* (1950). He was an embittered paraplegic, the first in a string of roles in which he played inarticulate and frequently violent characters: in the 1951 film of *Streetcar* (directed, as it was on Broadway, by Elia Kazan); *Viva Zapata!* (1952) as the Mexican revolutionary; *The Wild One* (1954), complete with peaked cap and leathers as the leader of a bike gang; and, outstandingly, Kazan's *On The Waterfront* (1954), an Oscar-winning performance as a washed-up boxer victimised by crooked union bosses, and the movie in which he gave utterance to one of the cinema's most oft-quoted lines, 'I coulda been a contender.' To escape from the stereotype of mumbling rebellion he then set about demonstrating his virtuosity: as a well thought out Mark Antony, co-starring with one of the world's best-spoken classical actors, John Gielgud, in *Julius Caesar* (1953); singing and dancing as Sky Masterson in *Guys And Dolls* (1955);

as a comic Japanese interpreter in *The Teahouse Of The August Moon* (1956); as a romantic lead in *Sayonara* (1957); and a blonde, idealistic German officer in *The Young Lions* (1958). Much of this was achieved by deploying an immense battery of technical tricks – a tendency he shares with Laurence Olivier – and today it is difficult to watch *On The Waterfront* without being distracted by the mechanics of Brando's performance. Nevertheless, in the 50s he could do no wrong.

The 60s were less happy, however. There were some good things: a directing debut in *One-Eyed Jacks* (1961); The persecuted lawman in *The Chase* (1966); and the homosexual army officer in *Reflections In A Golden Eye* (1967). But these were outweighed by a succession of disasters. Among them were *Mutiny On The Bounty* (1962), in which he tried to reinvent Clark Gable as a prissy Englishman, and Charlie Chaplin's *A Countess From Hong Kong* (1967). He redeemed himself in *The Godfather* (1972), giving a minutely observed impersonation of the aging Don Corleone, winning a second Oscar, and sending an Indian woman to collect it as a political gesture. He was an ex-prizefighter again in *Last Tango In Paris* (1972), a film of great sexual frankness, and mesmerising as the blubbery, dandified psychopath Robert E. Clayton in *The Missouri Breaks*. In *Superman* (1978) he took the money – over $2.5 million for a 10-minute cameo – and ran. However, he seemed uneasy in *Apocalypse Now* (1979), lurking in the shadows muttering 'The horror, the horror'. Another quirky cameo in *The Formula* (1980) suggests that he is reluctant to extend himself when so much is on offer for so little.

with Eva Marie Saint in *On The Waterfront*

AUDREY HEPBURN

AUDREY HEPBURN

Real name **Edda Hepburn van Heemstra**
Born **Brussels, Belgium, 4 May 1929**

In the early 1950s Audrey Hepburn stepped out of a *Vogue* fashion plate to entrance cinema audiences. She had all the mannequin elegance of Barbara Goalen and elfin eyes so expressive that it hardly seemed necessary for her to speak at all. The word gamine might have been invented for her, and there was a delicious whisper of other-worldliness in the free and innocent spirits she so often played, closer to the woods and glades of Arden than the hills of Beverly.

Born in Brussels in 1929 of Irish-Dutch parentage, she spent the war years in Holland, then moved to England to study with the Ballet Rambert. She returned to Holland for her screen debut, as an air stewardess, in *Nederland In 7 Lessen* (1948), played in revue in London and was signed by Associated British for a walk-on in an Alastair Sim comedy, *Laughter In Paradise* (1951). After a bigger part in *Young Wives' Tale* (1952), she was wanly touching as Valentina Cortese's ballerina sister in *Secret People* (1952), a political thriller. While filming in France she was taken up by Colette and shot to fame on Broadway in the title role of 'Gigi'. Paramount snapped her up for *Roman Holiday* (1954), as the incognito princess who runs off with reporter Gregory Peck, and the Academy awarded her a rather generous Best Actress Oscar. Billy Wilder played artfully on her coltish beauty and faintly sing-song voice in *Sabrina* (1954) with William Holden and Humphrey Bogart, then King Vidor cast her as Natasha in *War And Peace* (1956) — he claimed that no one else was considered for the part — and photographed her ravishingly in his Reader's Digest version of Tolstoy. Fred Astaire was lined up for her in the chic, Gershwin-scored

Funny Face (1957), transforming her from dowdy little bookseller to top fashion model. Naturally she looked divine, both before and after, and the film was a big hit. She was less successfully wooed by Gary Cooper in *Love In The Afternoon* (1957), then found herself in holy orders, and in the Belgian Congo, in *The Nun's Story* (1959). Unwisely, she declined *The Inn Of The Sixth Happiness* (1958), choosing instead the part of Rima the Bird Girl in *Green Mansions* (1959), a muddled version of W. H. Hudson's novel directed by her then husband Mel Ferrer. (She divorced him to marry an Italian psychiatrist named, amusingly to English ears, Dr Andrea Dotti, and made her home in Rome.) Far better was a John Huston Western, *The Unforgiven* (1960), in which she was a young woman coming to terms with her Indian blood. As Holly Golightly in *Breakfast At Tiffany's* (1961) — a part originally intended for Marilyn Monroe — she was overly winsome, crooning 'Moon River' to a bemused George Peppard. After *The Children's Hour* (1962), *Charade* (1963) and *Paris When It Sizzles* (1964), she proved that she was still box-office as Eliza Doolittle in *My Fair Lady* (1964) though, sadly, her quirky little voice was dubbed.

As youth ebbed away, so did her career. *After Two For The Road* (1967), a wry comedy of marriage in which she co-starred with Albert Finney, and *Wait Until Dark* (1967), she went into semi-retirement. She returned as an exquisitely aging Maid Marian in *Robin And Marian* (1976) opposite Sean Connery who was rather less exquisite as Robin Hood; and then for reasons best known to herself played the glamorous head of a multinational in the appalling *Bloodline* (1979).

with Peter Finch in The Nun's Story

BRIGITTE BARDOT

BRIGITTE BARDOT

*Born **Paris, France, 28 September 1934***

She lingers in the memory opulently naked in *La Vérité* (1960) and *Contempt* (1963), casually displaying her perfect body in sumptuous repose, tastefully placed drapes trailing over creamy breasts and neatly boyish bottom. She had a devastating pout, like a naughty but very knowing little girl, and her smile was an open invitation to all stray males. She was born into a well-to-do Parisian family, became a popular model by the time she was 16 and was spotted on the cover of *Elle* magazine by a young assistant director, Roger Vadim. Two years later they were married and, Svengali-like, Vadim set about inventing BB, the sultry symbol of beckoning post-war affluence and sexual permissiveness.

She flitted in and out of a string of French movies until an appearance as a handmaiden in *Helen Of Troy* (1955) prompted Warners to offer her a contract. She declined, but in the same year she was brought over to Britain for Rank to add an exotic touch to *Doctor At Sea* (1955), starring Dirk Bogarde. She was still a brunette and still a supporting player, but within a year she had toppled Martine Carol as France's leading sex symbol and, in 1957, became an international star in Vadim's *And God Created Woman*. Blonde now, she played fast and loose in St Tropez, soon to become the ultra-fashionable playground where paparazzi vied with each other to record the more public episodes in her stimulating private life, including her divorce from Vadim. Shortly afterwards and while Columbia haggled over a three-picture deal, she starred with Charles Boyer in *Une Parisienne* (1957); in *Love Is My Profession* (1958) she signalled her sexual candour by lifting up her skirts to show Jean Gabin

that she was most definitely not wearing knickers, while *Babette Goes to War* (1959) was a lame attempt to showcase her in comedy as a plucky Resistance girl sent by the British to kidnap a German General.

But the strain of being the world's Number One Sex Kitten was beginning to tell, seeming to sap her vitality. In recent photographs, her eyes seem like dark slits in a pale mask, stretched ever tighter by age. In and out of love and marriage, and the subject of a particularly idiotic book by Simone de Beauvoir, she tried to kill herself while filming *La Vérité*. The Hollywood majors resolved to keep their distance, until MGM financed *La Vie Privée* (1962), a confused attempt to examine her own legend as a sex symbol. She finally acquired an American co-star, the hapless Anthony Perkins, in *Une Ravissante Idiote* (1963) and, in the same year, appeared briefly, as herself, in a James Stewart comedy *Dear Brigitte*. She was teamed with Jeanne Moreau for *Viva Maria* (1965), a film given a vast publicity build-up, but she seemed to be completely thrown by her co-star's angular beauty and reputation. Subsequently, more column inches were devoted to the lovers she took than the films she made (in recent years these have been replaced by animal welfare causes for which she is a deeply committed and tireless worker), although *Shalako* (1968) was a serviceable spaghetti Western and *L'Ours Et La Poupée* (1970) achieved a modest commercial success in France. In international terms, however, she was a busted flush. Vadim returned in 1973 to direct *Don Juan* in a sad attempt to orchestrate Bardot and Jane Birkin into bed, but the results singularly failed to scorch the sheets.

with Franco Interlenghi in *Love Is My Profession*

GENE KELLY

GENE KELLY

Real name **Eugene Curran Kelly**
Born **Pittsburgh, Pennsylvania, 23 August 1912**

Inevitably the comparison is always made with Astaire. Fred glides across the set with the thoughtless grace which conceals the perfectionist beneath. Gene is chunky, an Ordinary Joe with a ready grin and tree-trunk thighs whose athleticism is tempered by romantic aspirations which occasionally hover on the edge of pretentiousness. Fred gives little away while Kelly is wide-open and bravura, the bristling energy contrasting pleasingly with the slight sense of strain in his light voice.

He came comparatively late to the movies, aged 30, after starring on Broadway as Joey Evans in 'Pal Joey'. MGM cast him as a similar heel-hero in *For Me And My Gal* (1942), a film animated by the magical rapport between Kelly and co-star Judy Garland. The 'Mop Dance' in *Thousands Cheer* (1943) was an early indication of his inventiveness, as was the 'alter ego' sequence in *Cover Girl* (1944), in which he capers with his own reflection. *Anchors Aweigh* (1945) contains an exuberant swashbuckling routine, a sketch for *The Pirate* (1948), a blaze of colour and frenzied dancing calculated to accommodate his masculine swagger. His next film was *The Three Musketeers* (1948), as the most dashing of D'Artagnans. With Vera-Ellen he was the best thing in *Words And Music* (1948), dancing 'Slaughter On Tenth Avenue'. Then came *On The Town* (1949), co-directed with Stanley Donen. With its balletic inspiration and location shooting — and boasting a superbly gifted and exuberant cast including Frank Sinatra, Ann Miller and Vera Ellen — it remains the freshest musical of the decade, much imitated in the early 50s but never bettered. After dancing with a newspaper and a squeaky floorboard in

Summer Stock (1950), Kelly made his most ambitious musical, *An American In Paris* (1951), which climaxed in a 20-minute ballet inspired by the work of the Impressionists. Among the film's eight Oscars was a special award for Kelly as dancer and choreographer. *Singin' In The Rain* (1952) shows him at his most versatile, contriving another complex ballet, danced with the exquisite Cyd Charisse, and doing the simple thing perfectly with a lamp post, an umbrella and a shower of rain.

The rest of his career reverberates with anti-climax, including *Brigadoon* (1954) and *It's Always Fair Weather* (1955), dancing and singing 'I Like Myself' on rollerskates. *Les Girls* (1957) was his last major musical, since when he has been seen only infrequently as a dancer: touchingly as a *passé* hoofer in *What A Way To Go* (1964); nervously stretching aging legs in *Les Demoiselles de Rochefort*; and in the frightful *Xanadu* (1980). His career as a straight actor has been uneven. He was not at ease as Deanna Durbin's ne'er-do-well husband in *Christmas Holiday* (1944) nor as Natalie Wood's Jewish boyfriend in *Marjorie Morningstar* (1958). He fared better as a reporter in *Inherit The Wind* (1960), and achieved a Best Supporting Actor nomination for Neil Simon's *Forty Carats* (1973). When not in motion a certain heartlessness lurks behind the genial exterior — even in *Singin' In The Rain* his grinning exposure of Jean Hagen's Bronx accent leaves a sour taste in an otherwise joyous movie. As a director, he is notable for *Hello Dolly* (1968) and *The Cheyenne Social Club* (1970), a comedy Western in which he skilfully manipulated the charm of its two elderly stars, Henry Fonda and James Stewart.

in *Singin' In The Rain*

SUSAN HAYWARD

SUSAN HAYWARD

Real name **Edythe Marrener**
Born **Brooklyn, New York, 30 June 1918**
Died **1975**

Pugnacity is the key to Susan Hayward's screen personality, a quality already evident in an early studio cheesecake shot in which the chubby young hopeful poses in a swimsuit, wielding a bow and arrow aimed straight at the camera. Her determination and directness — which grew more strident with the passage of time — made her one of the more resistible of Hollywood's leading ladies but ensured that she stayed on screen, socking it to us, almost to the very end.

She began as a dress designer, then modelling led her to screen tests for the part of Scarlett O'Hara in *Gone With The Wind* (1939) (along with almost every other faintly glamorous, fairly competent actress in Hollywood), and the subsequent firm set of her jaw hints at the trouper who remained convinced that she should have got the part. Her first movie was a Ronald Reagan B, *Girls On Probation* (1938). Thereafter she was frequently cast as a bright, eager young thing, decorating actioners like *Beau Geste* (1939) and *Reap The Wild Wind* (1942). But she was much better playing bitches, in *Among The Living* (1941), *Adam Had Four Sons* (1941) and *The Hairy Ape* (1944), from Eugene O'Neill's drama, in which she was the well-bred object of William Bendix's coarse attentions. She soldiered on until *Deadline At Dawn* showed her gritty streak, clearing sailor Bill Williams of a murder rap. Then in *Smash-Up, The Story Of A Woman* (1947) she unleashed her capacity for suffering as the alcoholic wife of songwriter Lee Bowman. She hit the bottle again, though rather more romantically, in *My Foolish Heart* (1949) — a big hit — then clawed her way to the top of the garment trade in *I Can Get It For You Wholesale* (1951). She hit her stride in the early 50s, perfectly at home in the gaudy absurdities of spear and sandal epics like *David And Bathsheba* (1951) and *Demetrius And The Gladiators* (1954); or vigorously bringing modern medicine to African tribesmen in *White Witch Doctor* (1953). Nicholas Ray cleverly exploited her natural aggressiveness in *The Lusty Men* (1952) as a rodeo rider's wife battling to preserve a stable home life. The suffering was piled on that year in *With A Song In My Heart,* a biopic of the singer Jane Froman who was crippled in a 'plane crash. In *I'll Cry Tomorrow* (1955) she sank her teeth into portraying, in another show biz weepie, the alcoholic singer Lillian Roth. Three years later she was at her gutsiest in *I Want to Live* (1958), winning an academy award as the prostitute-crook Barbara Graham, framed for murder and agonisedly waiting on Death Row for the gas chamber.

After an insipid remake of *Back Street* (1961) she moved on to *grande dame* roles. *Stolen Hours* (1963) was a remake of *Dark Victory* (1939), a weepie originally crafted for Bette Davis, who turned up as her mother in *Where Love Has Gone* (1964). She was a last-minute replacement for Judy Garland in *Valley Of The Dolls* (1967) and waded through the trash with fierce, unmodulated intensity. But there was a touching note of tenderness in *The Revengers* (1972) as she hesitantly offered herself to William Holden. She died in 1975 after a long battle with cancer, thought to have been contracted while filming *The Conqueror* (1956) on location in the Nevada Desert which still housed radiation from A-Bomb tests. The ravishing, husky-voiced redhead was only 56 years old.

with Robert Mitchum in *The Lusty Men*

DIRK BOGARDE

DIRK BOGARDE

Real name **Derek Van Den Bogaerde**
Born **London, England, 28 March 1920**

Dirk Bogarde, who began his long film career as the male equivalent of a Rank charm school starlet, is probably the finest camera actor in the world today. Sensitivity, control and reticence are the hallmarks of his elegant style. He became a star in the early 50s – the last era of the manufactured movie idol – and the air of the old-fashioned star still clings to him, an impression underlined by his studied refusal to do television work.

Born in London in 1920, he was a commercial artist before going on to the stage. He returned to the theatre after war service and was then cast as the ne'er-do-well footman William Latch in *Esther Waters* (1948). The next year he had a big success as the hysterical young hoodlum Tom Riley in *The Blue Lamp* (1949), bungling a stick-up, panicking, and plugging avuncular policeman Jack Warner. Thereafter Bogarde had the singular misfortune to become one of the leading men in British cinema. In *The Blue Lamp* he had displayed a sensual streak markedly at odds with the bluff style of contemporaries but, over the next ten years, it surfaced only intermittently, in *The Sleeping Tiger* – his first collaboration with Joseph Losey – *The Spanish Gardener* (1956) and *The Singer Not The Song* (1961), in which he deliberately camped it up as a Mexican bandit encased in black leather. For the rest, Bogarde applied himself to smooth interpretations of comedy, notably as Simon Sparrow in four 'Doctor' films, costume adventure, and that staple of British cinema of the 50s, the war film, including *They Who Dare* (1954), *The Sea Shall Not Have Them* (1954), and the quirky *III Met By Moonlight* (1957). He survived the idiocies of *Song Without End* (1961), playing Liszt with a romantic flourish, and then

took a great risk as the homosexual barrister in *Victim* (1961). In his own words he was no longer the 'bouncy, happy doctor with a little perm in the front lock of my hair and my caps in and every set built for my left profile.' All his natural tact was required in co-starring with Judy Garland in *I Could Go On Singing* (1963) and then he was re-united with Losey for *The Servant* (1963), giving a portrayal of chilling malice which finally buried the matinée idol image and established him as a character actor of international reputation. There was more with Losey – *King And Country* (1964), *Accident* (1967), and *Modesty Blaise* (1966), in which Bogarde displayed his flair for comedy, playing Gabriel, one of the decade's most stylish villains, sporting a silver wig and sipping cocktails from a glass the size of a goldfish bowl, complete with goldfish.

Bogarde began the 70s with a mesmerising technical *tour de force* in Visconti's *Death In Venice* (1971). After Liliana Cavani's *The Night Porter* (1973), in which he starred opposite Charlotte Rampling, his appearances became less frequent. Not surprisingly, perhaps since the film itself, which concerned the obsessive sexual relationship between a concentration camp overseer and one of his female inmates, turned out to be tasteless in the extreme. He lives in France, a somewhat aloof figure, devoting much time to writing. His fastidious temperament has undoubtedly narrowed the range of roles open to him, but he was excellent in Alain Resnais' *Providence* (1977), rekindled memories of his 50s war films in *A Bridge Too Far* (1977), and collaborated with director Rainer Fassbinder in *Despair* (1978).

with Brigitte Bardot in *Doctor At Sea*

DEBORAH KERR

DEBORAH KERR

Real name **Deborah Kerr-Trimmer**
Born **Helensburgh, Scotland, 30 September 1921**

Hollywood has always reserved a pedestal for stately British leading ladies, cool and graceful actresses under whose gentility there might just lurk a streak of sensuality. First Diana Wynyard and then Greer Garson personified the ladylike virtues, and in 1945 Louis B. Mayer signed the 24-year-old Deborah Kerr as the next in line. She had made her screen debut in *Contraband* (1940), in a cameo which ended up on the cutting room floor. After *Major Barbara* (1941) she starred in *Love On The Dole* (1941), struggling with a North Country accent which smacked more of Surbiton than Salford. She came into her own in Michael Powell's *The Life And Death Of Colonel Blimp* (1943), red-haired and ravishing as the three women in Roger Livesey's life. MGM signed her to co-star with Robert Donat in *Perfect Strangers*, which was followed by a seven-year contract. After two loan-outs – charming as a fiery young Irish girl in *I See A Dark Stranger* (1946) and singularly beautiful as a nun in *Black Narcissus* (1947) – she went to Hollywood for *The Hucksters* (1947) with Clark Gable. She suffered nobly in *If Winter Comes* (1947), finding last-reel happiness with Walter Pidgeon, and was driven into a state of genteel alcoholism by Spencer Tracy in *Edward My Son* (1949). Melodrama gave way to a string of adventure films – *King Solomon's Mines* (1950), *Quo Vadis?* (1951) and *The Prisoner Of Zenda* (1952) – in which she was required to be little more than decorative.

The turning point came in *From Here To Eternity* (1953), when she abandoned restraint to play the sexually frustrated wife taking an illicit tumble in the surf with Burt Lancaster. Nevertheless, she still retained the air of a memsahib unaccountably called upon to comfort the soldiery in Honolulu. She was unfaithful again, poignantly this time, in *The End Of The Affair* (1955), was seduced by brutal William Holden in *The Proud And The Profane* (1955) and then whistled a happy tune as the resourceful governess in *The King And I* (1956). In *Tea And Sympathy* she generously offered herself to John Kerr (he's worried that he might by gay) and then played another nun, shipwrecked on a desert island with lusty Robert Mitchum in *Heaven Knows, Mr Allison* (1957). Otto Preminger found a sharper edge to her overwhelming niceness in *Bonjour Tristesse* (1958), but she was less happy in the screen version of Terence Rattigan's *Separate Tables* (1958) as a dowdy spinster, and in the misconceived biopic, *Beloved Infidel* (1959) as Scott Fitzgerald's mistress, Sheila Graham, opposite an equally unhappy Gregory Peck.

Reunited with Mitchum in *The Sundowners* (1960) she gave a touching performance as an Australian sheepherder's wife, but the next ten years saw her in an odd mixture of ambitious failures and out-and-out rubbish. Into the first category fell her performances as the spinster governess in *The Innocents* (1962) and the abandoned wife in *The Arrangement* (1970). In the second were *Marriage On The Rocks* (1965), *Eye Of The Devil* (1965) and *Prudence And The Pill* (1968). She emerged with some credit from *The Gypsy Moths* (1969) and was excellent in another spinster role in *Night Of The Iguana* (1964). After a long stint in the theatre she returned successfully to the screen, playing the part of an elderly relic of the British Raj in *The Assam Garden* (1985).

with John Kerr in *Tea And Sympathy*

JAMES STEWART

JAMES STEWART

*Born **Indiana, Pennsylvania, 20 May 1908***

In the late 30s James Stewart's screen image was fixed as the wide-eyed country boy whose gangling innocence put the sophisticates and schemers to rout in Frank Capra's *Mr Smith Goes To Washington* (1939). The character he played in that film, Jefferson Smith, combined a soft-spoken sincerity, a touching physical awkwardness and a drawling flair for populist oratory which made Stewart one of the most trusted of movie actors, the embodiment of provincial naturalism and All-American virtue.

As the director W.S. Van Dyke observed, 'he was so unusually usual.' In 1940 he reached the peak of the first phase in his career, winning the Best Actor Oscar for *The Philadelphia Story* and starring on Broadway in 'Harvey' as Elwood P. Dowd, the gentle fantasist befriended by a giant invisible rabbit (he starred in the film in 1950). After loving and losing Lana Turner in *Ziegfeld Girls* (1941) he joined the USAAF, returning to Hollywood in 1946 after distinguished war service (he remains a general), and spent the rest of the 40s as a freelance. The small-town sentimentality of *It's A Wonderful Life* (1947) and *Magic Town* (1947) were out of step with the postwar demand for a measure of realism, a path Stewart trod in *Call Northside 777* (1948), a hard-hitting melodrama. After his first film with Alfred Hitchcock, *Rope* (1948), *The Stratton Story* (1949), an inspirational baseball biopic, and *Malaya* (1949), a leaden actioner, he went to Universal for *Winchester 73* (1950) with Anthony Mann and to Fox for *Broken Arrow* (1950) with Delmer Daves. The success of these two Westerns was crucial to the second stage in his career, leading to a contract with Universal with a percentage of his films' profits,

and a fruitful association with Anthony Mann. In *Bend Of The River* (1952), *Thunder Bay* (1953) and *The Naked Spur* (1954) Mann began to tinker with Stewart's open, sunny disposition, presenting a more tetchy, complicated figure, a man wrestling with suppressed malevolence, often isolated in a harsh landscape and the victim of calculately brutal violence. The old charm resurfaced unscathed in *The Glenn Miller Story* (1954) a superior example of the biopic and a huge hit, and his fine war record was invoked in *Strategic Air Command* (1955). But Hitchcock gleefully pounced on Stewart's new personality in *Rear Window* (1954) with Grace Kelly, *The Man Who Knew Too Much* (1955) with Doris Day, and *Vertigo* (1958) with Kim Novak. In the middle of this fertile period came Mann's *The Man From Laramie*, a taut revenge Western in which Stewart hunted down the men who killed his brothers. After the commercial failure of *The Spirit Of St Louis* (1957) – in which he played Lindbergh – the tension relaxed. *Bell, Book And Candle* (1958) marked a return to whimsical comedy. In *Anatomy Of A Murder* (1959) he was Mr Smith grown up into a deceptively easygoing country lawyer.

Thereafter he seemed content to subside into self-indulgent gestures towards his pre-war successes. John Ford encouraged this in *The Man Who Shot Liberty Valance* (1962) and Gene Kelly exploited it in *The Cheyenne Social Club* (1970). However, Robert Aldrich slyly caught him unawares as the elderly pilot in *The Flight Of The Phoenix* (1965). And Don Siegel gave him the poignant task – in view of its offscreen truth – of telling John Wayne that he had cancer in *The Shootist* (1976).

in Thunder Bay

LESLIE CARON

L E S L I E   C A R O N

Born **Boulogne-Billancourt, France, 1 July 1931**

Leslie Caron was born near Paris to a French father and an American mother, herself a former dancer. She trained as a ballerina and was spotted by Gene Kelly dancing in 'La Rencontre' with the Ballets des Champs Elysees. In her movie debut in *An American In Paris* (1951), the taut concentration of the classical dancer makes her seem a little stiff and preoccupied. With time and experience the tension fell away and her beauty shone through. But she has always remained conscientious and serious, and it is difficult to imagine Caron really letting herself go.

After a brief period as a Beverly Hills beatnik she settled down to play the studio game. *Glory Alley* (1952) was an old-fashioned boxing melodrama in which she danced very sexily. In *Lili* (1953) she was cast as a gauche teenage orphan – a role she virtually copyrighted in the 50s – who becomes a waitress in a carnival and awakens love in crippled, self-pitying puppeteer Mel Ferrer. It is a performance of great charm in a film which slides inexorably into sentimentality. She rapidly overtook the ill-fated Pier Angeli as MGM's leading continental import, co-starring with Farley Granger in *The Story Of Three Loves* (1953) and tactfully guiding an uneasy Michael Wilding through the ballet sequences in *The Glass Slipper* (1954). She was an orphan again in *Daddy Long Legs* (1954), falling for wealthy benefactor Fred Astaire and dancing sweetly with him in 'Something's Gotta Give'. Then came a real clinker, *Gaby* (1956), a *Waterloo Bridge* retread with John Kerr. In London she played the lead in 'Gigi' in the West End, married director Peter Hall (now Sir Peter and on his third wife) and declined to return to Hollywood until MGM decided to film the show. They wanted Audrey Hepburn, but Caron was still under contract and cheaper. Costumed by Cecil Beaton, directed by Vincente Minnelli and suavely romanced by Louis Jourdan, the gamine blossomed into a handsome, poised woman.

The Oscar-bedecked *Gigi* (1958) was the last of the great MGM musicals and Caron's subsequent career has lacked any discernible direction. A capable performance opposite Dirk Bogarde in *The Doctor's Dilemma* (1959) was followed by the feeble *The Man Who Understood Women* (1959) and *The Subterraneans* (1960). She was now too old for orphans, so she acquired an illegitimate child instead in *Fanny* (1961) and *The L-Shaped Room* (1964), an old-fashioned British boarding house drama given a lick of contemporary social realism. Hollywood tried her out in three prim comedy roles in *Father Goose* (1964), *A Very Special Favour* (1965) and *Promise Her Anything* (1966). The object of the exercise was to watch her melt, but somehow she failed to do so. She was one of the best things in *Is Paris Burning?* (1966) and then, after an unsuccessful assault on Hollywood in the early 70s, returned to Paris for *Serail* (1976), as a severe housekeeper. Ken Russell cast her somewhat unwisely as the great Russian actress Nazimova in *Valentino* (1977), a project best forgotten by all concerned, and she returned to Hollywood two years later for a supporting role in *Golden Girl* (1979). Leslie Caron somehow remains defiantly lodged in the public consciousness as a star – which in the 50s she undoubtedly was – but, alas, she has by now all but vanished from the firmament.

with Fred Astaire in *Daddy Long Legs*

WILLIAM HOLDEN

WILLIAM HOLDEN

Real name **William Franklin Beedle, Jr**
Born **O'Fallon, Illinois, 17 April 1918**
Died **1981**

In the 1950s he was known in the business as 'Golden Holden', a supremely reliable and bankable star, ruggedly good-looking in a commonplace kind of way – a handsome version of the guy who came to mend the television set or served you at the gas station. He had a no-nonsense attitude towards acting, claiming he didn't like it very much, which endeared him to director Billy Wilder: 'He is the ideal motion picture actor. He is beyond acting . . . You never doubt or question what he is. Jimmy Stewart is the prime example of that kind of actor. So is Gary Cooper. There is no crap about them'.

Signed by Paramount in 1937, he remained inactive for two years before being loaned out to star in Columbia's *Golden Boy* (1939) as the boxer who really wants to be a concert violinist. It was a good start, and in unpretentious films like *The Remarkable Andrew* (1942), *Apartment For Peggy* (1947) and *Rachel And The Stranger* (1948) he showed that he had plenty of relaxed, boyish charm, although he lacked the incisiveness to impose himself on a film. Billy Wilder was the first to chart the shifting sands beneath the plausible surface. In *Sunset Boulevard* (1950), Wilder's masterpiece about a faded silent star, he was Joe Gillis, the would-be screenwriter who narrates the film while floating face downwards in Gloria Swanson's swimming pool. In between a tedious run of routine outings, several of them co-starring the anodyne Nancy Olson, Wilder used Holden skilfully as a stooge for the gifted Judy Holliday in *Born Yesterday* (1950) and then coaxed an impressively bad-tempered performance from him in *Stalag 17* (1953), as the prison camp black

marketeer suspected of being a German stool pigeon. He won a Best Actor Oscar and moved up to bigger roles with his name above the title, but nowadays he seems dull as a romantic lead in *Sabrina* (1954) or *Love Is A Many-Splendoured Thing* (1955). He was more effective as a predator in *The Moon Is Blue* (1953); as a heel in *Picnic* (1956); as an extremely reluctant hero in *The Bridge On The River Kwai* (1957). This last film propelled him into the salary stratosphere, and for *The Horse Soldiers* (1959), with John Wayne, he got $750,000 with 20 per cent of the profits. Not surprisingly, after a torpid run of films in the 60s, *Variety* voted him one of 1968's most overpriced stars.

He was middle-aged now, eyes sinking deeper into his skull and worry lines seaming his face – perfect for the role of the aging outlaw leader in *The Wild Bunch* (1969). He reprised the performance, in muted style, in *Wild Rovers* (1971) and *The Revengers* (1972), was the unfortunate architect responsible for *The Towering Inferno* (1974) and the dyspeptic real estate man snared by teenage hippy Kay Lenz in *Breezy* (1975). He adopted an appropriately serious air as the anchor-man in *Network* (1976) – a sentimental and somewhat overrated film, starring Peter Finch and Faye Dunaway – but was much more interesting as a washed-up movie producer (a sort of Joe Gillis, 60 and disillusioned) in Wilder's *Fedora* (1978), an intriguingly botched companion piece to *Sunset Boulevard*. He had a mild success in his last film, *S.O.B.* (1981), but died in the same year, falling in his apartment after a solitary drinking session and bleeding to death. His body lay undiscovered for several days.

with Judy Holliday in Born Yesterday

AVA GARDNER

A V A   G A R D N E R

*Born **Smithfield, North Carolina, 24 January 1922***

In *The Barefoot Contessa* (1954), a film whose plot somewhat mirrors her own life (she was born in North Carolina, one of the six children of a poor tenant farmer), she plays a Spanish gypsy girl who becomes a screen goddess. Confiding in director Humphrey Bogart, she tells him, 'I think I'm pretty, but I don't want to be that kind of star'. She was wrong on both counts. 'Pretty' does scant justice to Ava Gardner's dark Latin beauty, her steady, sensual stare, the feline carriage and the adventuress' barely concealed air of contempt for the more drab mortals around her. And, inevitably perhaps, Hollywood reduced her to just 'that kind of star', smothering the languorous sexuality under several layers of studio gloss.

She was spotted as a teenager while staying with her photographer brother-in-law in New York. MGM signed her up and hurried her through a string of Bs, but at the time she was better known as Mrs Mickey Rooney, a marriage partly engineered by the studio's remorseless publicity machine. A press agent accompanied the young couple on their honeymoon. She had moved on to husband number 2, bandleader Artie Shaw, when the big break came. In *The Killers* (1946) she struck sparks off another newcomer, Burt Lancaster, and the studio moved her up to bigger roles in *The Hucksters* with Clark Gable (1947), *Singapore* (1947), *One Touch Of Venus* (1948) and *The Gambler* (1949). In MGM's technicolor remake of *Showboat* (1951), her touching portrayal of the half-caste Julie was compromised by the dubbing of 'Can't Help Lovin' Dat Man'. *Pandora And the Flying Dutchman* (1951) – a lush, idiotic exercise in mythology co-starring James Mason and now becoming a cult movie – showcased her

lustrous beauty, while in *Mogambo*. John Ford's remake of *Red Dust* (1932), she gave a sultry twist to Jean Harlow's original role. It was a part that marked a watershed in her career.

By then stormily married to Frank Sinatra – a liaison in which frequent absences signally failed to make tht heart grow fonder – she spent more time in Europe than Hollywood, complaining loudly about MGM and consoling herself with the attentions of adoring bullfighters. Not surprisingly for an aficionado of matadors she became a Hemingway woman in *The Snows Of Kilimanjaro* (1952) and *The Sun Also Rises* (1957). But her two best performances came in *The Barefoot Contessa*, in which Joseph Mankiewicz skilfully manipulated her narrow range, and *Bhowani Junction* (1956), again playing a half-caste. After *On The Beach* (1959) her work became more sporadic. In *Fifty-Five Days At Peking* (1963) she crossed the threshold of middle age but still looked stunning. *Night Of The Iguana* (1964), from Tennessee Williams' play, the only film she claims to have enjoyed making (it was certainly the heavyweight entry in her filmography), gave her the chance to play an Earth Mother in the company of Richard Burton and Deborah Kerr. In the offbeat *Devil's Widow* (1971) she resorted to witchcraft to keep her looks, although the evidence of more recent outings in *The Sentinel* (1977) and *City On Fire* (1979) shows that she needn't worry over much. As Edmond O'Brien observes in *The Barefoot Contessa* (1954), 'Whatever it is, whether you are born with it, or catch it from a public drinking cup, she's got it and the people with the money in their hands put her there'.

with Grace Kelly in *Mogambo*

KIRK DOUGLAS

KIRK DOUGLAS

Real name **Issur Danielovitch**
Born **Amsterdam, New York, 9 December 1916**

At the beginning of the actor's career producer Hal Wallis considered filling in the cavernous cleft in his chin. It was as forlorn a hope as MGM's attempt to pin back Clark Gable's ears. The ferocious movie landmark, and the stonecracking grin, are the outward manifestations of Kirk Douglas' driving energy, burning at its brightest in the midst of agony and mutilation. He was beaten to a pulp in *Champion* (1949); fatally stabbed with a pair of scissors in *Ace In The Hole* (1951); rolled up in barbed wire in *Man Without A Star* (1955) and crucified in *Spartacus* (1960). Various parts of his anatomy have littered the set: a finger in *The Big Sky* (1952); an ear in *Lust for Life* (1956); and an eye in *The Vikings* (1958). Clearly he enjoys it – perhaps it's the Russian in him.

Wallis signed Douglas shortly after the war and he made his debut, as Barbara Stanwyck's alcoholic husband, in *The Strange Love Of Martha Ivers* (1946). He attracted attention as a gangster in *Out Of The Past* (1947), the first of many roles as a ruthless, grinning schemer, and broke through to stardom as the unscrupulous fighter in *Champion*. Warner Bros. snapped him up on a seven-year contract and pushed him through *Young Man With A Horn* (1950), as Bix Beiderbecke, and *The Glass Menagerie* (1951), as The Gentleman Caller. But he was at his best in grindingly egotistical roles: as the heartless newsman in Billy Wilder's *Ace In The Hole*; or the ambitious movie producer in *The Bad And The Beautiful* (1952). Nice guys and subtlety lay outside his range, but his intensity made suffering credible in *Along The Great Divide* (1952), *Detective Story* (1951) and *Lust For Life*, as the tormented Vincent Van Gogh. To relax, he enjoyed himself hugely playing flamboyant, crackpot villains hovering on the edge of parody: Captain Nemo in *20,000 Leagues Under The Sea* (1954), and the one-eyed heavy in *The Vikings*. He reined himself in for Kubrick's *Paths Of Glory* (1957), giving an exceptionally well-judged performance as an idealistic World War I French officer caught in the cynical toils of general staff politics. He was the obvious choice as the slave hero of the epic *Spartacus*, but was much better used in a small, underrated film – David Miller's *Lonely Are The Brave*, a contemporary Western. After *Two Weeks In Another Town* (1962), in which he was characteristically sharp-edged as a has-been film director, his outline became increasingly blurred in a string of flaccid actioners including the starry but incoherent *The List Of Adrian Messenger* (1963), *The Heroes Of Telemark* (1965) and *The War Wagon* (1967).

Given a meaty role in *The Arrangement* (1968), written and directed by Elia Kazan from his own bestselling novel, he overbalanced into pretentiousness. He made a welcome return to his old bravura style in *A Gunfight* (1971), as an aging pistolero arranging a grandstand finish to his career, but was less successful playing against type as a wimpish murderer in *Cat And Mouse* (1974) and bursting out of the part as if it was a suit several sizes too small for him. He was his old urgent self again in *The Fury* (1978), a science-fiction tinged thriller and, still working, ventured into SF again in *The Final Countdown* (1980). The successful producer (*One Flew Over The Cuckoo's Nest*, 1975, was his debut effort) and film actor, Michael Douglas, is his son.

in *The Vikings*

GRACE KELLY

GRACE KELLY

Born *Philadelphia, Pennsylvania, 12 November 1928*
Died *1982*

The name Grace Kelly was always guaranteed to send grizzled hacks groping for the well-worn cliché of 'Fairytale Princess'. Princess she undoubtedly was, and no one has ever filled the part with such discreet elegance. She was born with a silver spoon in her mouth, the daughter of a wealthy Philadelphia industrialist, and enjoyed a privileged if somewhat strict Catholic upbringing. Uncle George had been a successful play-wright, so there were few objections when she went to study at The American Academy of Dramatic Art, making her Broadway debut as Raymond Massey's daughter in 'The Father'. Television brought her to the attention of 20th Century-Fox, who put her in *14 Hours* (1951), as one of the crowd waiting to see if would-be suicide Richard Basehart would jump off a window ledge (he didn't). She declined a contract but a year later played Gary Cooper's wife in *High Noon* (1952).

There was still little about her to suggest stardom and, in *Mogambo* (1953), Ava Gardner wiped the floor with her. It was Alfred Hitchcock who seized on her demure cool, casting her as the unfaithful wife in *Dial M For Murder* (1954). For Hitchcock, whose bulky frame hid a hothouse of sexual fantasies, Kelly was the perfect blonde – 'the drawing room type, the real lady, who becomes a whore in the bedroom'. In *Rear Window* (1954) she dripped well-bred class while posing teasingly in a nightgown, in front of James Stewart, and in *To Catch A Thief* (1955), she offered Cary Grant a chicken picnic and in the same breath enquired, 'breast or leg?'. *Rear Window* made her a star, and a dazzled Hollywood presented her with the Best Actress Oscar for her performance as Bing Crosby's dowdy,

embittered wife in *The Country Girl* (1954) – more probably earned, it must be said, for the impact of her unexpected image than because she could possibly have been thought to out-act fellow nominee Judy Garland in *A Star Is Born*. After *The Bridges At Toko-Ri* (1954), as William Holden's wife, and *Green Fire* (1955), a jungle adventure with MGM's resident white hunter Stewart Granger, MGM set about packaging her as they had Garbo and Ingrid Bergman in the 30s. However, it was a sign of the studio's fossilised imagination that they could only come up with remakes such as *The Swan* (1956), an interminable Ruritanian romance originally filmed by Lillian Gish, and *High Society* (1956), a musical version of *The Philadelphia Story* (1940), in which she was fine, provided you hadn't seen Katherine Hepburn in the original. (Bing Crosby subbed for Cary Grant.) She was spared the Norma Shearer role in *The Barretts Of Wimpole Street*, but by now all this was academic.

In 1955 she met Prince Rainier of Monaco at the Cannes Film Festival and married him in April of the following year. There were occasional teasing hints of a comeback. Hitchcock offered her *Marnie* (1964) – the part eventually went to another 'ice maiden', Tippi Hedren – but the Pope intervened, expressing the hope that she would set a good example to Catholic mothers everywhere by not leaving her children to return to work. But her last role was the one she played to perfection – the exquisitely coiffed and gracious Princess Grace, awarding prizes at the Monaco Grand Prix and compering charity concerts at which she occasionally read poetry. She died tragically in a car crash in 1982.

with James Stewart in *Rear Window*

BURT LANCASTER

BURT LANCASTER

Real name **Burton Stephen Lancaster**
Born **New York City, 2 November 1913**

Now in his seventies, Burt Lancaster still radiates strapping athleticism, the grin as fierce, the gaze as direct and penetrating as in the days when he swung dizzily through the rigging in *The Crimson Pirate* (1952). As David Thomson has observed, 'his vitality is more than cheerfulness or strength; he seems charged with power . . . his hand outstretched but with the hint that his grip could crush or galvanise.' He came to films via an early career as a circus acrobat and war service in North Africa. Signed by Hal Wallis, he made a smouldering debut in *The Killers* (1946), already suggesting the suppressed power which is his trademark. He quickly carved out a niche in hardnosed melodramas – *Brute Force* (1947), *Desert Fury* (1947), *Criss Cross* (1949). Then, in *Sorry, Wrong Number* (1949), as Barbara Stanwyck's treacherous husband, he showed his quality as a smiling villain – all polite attentiveness, with the menace curled up under the surface like a slumbering big cat. *The Flame And The Arrow* (1950) was his first swashbuckler, a carefree Technicolor romp in which Jacques Tourneur fashioned him into a Tuscan Robin Hood. Two years later, in *The Crimson Pirate*, he zestily outdid all the adventure clichés made famous by Fairbanks Sr. Years afterwards he recalled wistfully, 'they were fun days . . . we set the town on fire with every movie we made.'

His delight in spectacle, and his physical grace, have never deserted him and are the leitmotifs of many of his films: *Apache* (1954), *The Kentuckian* (1955), *The Train* (1964), *The Professionals* (1966), even *The Swimmer* (1967), a genuine curiosity in which he is a middle-aged man progressing from pool to pool in a suburban journey of self-discovery. As

an actor he found his feet in *Come Back Little Sheba* (1953), playing a barely reformed alcoholic. But he is at his audience-crunching best as a swaggering imposter pumped up on the juices of an inflamed ego: as the appalling gossip columnist J. J. Hunsecker in *Sweet Smell Of Success* (1957); or winning an Oscar as the charlatan evangelist in *Elmer Gantry* (1960), a brilliant exercise in the application of self-conscious charm. In more austere mood he was quietly moving as the lifer Robert Stroud, *The Birdman Of Alcatraz* (1962), while his Sicilian nobleman in Luchino Visconti's *The Leopard* (1963) – a film tragically mangled by 20th Century-Fox – is a magisterial performance and the peak of his career.

Like all the stars who came to the fore immediately after the war and who basked briefly in the brilliant setting sun of the studio empires, Burt Lancaster found it difficult to adjust to the changing fashions and economic imperatives of the 1960s and '70s. But that alchemist of a director Robert Altman extended him in *Ulzana's Raid*, as an aging scout tracking down just such a renegade Indian as he had played in *Apache*. Reunited with Visconti, he gave a well-judged performance in *Conversation Piece* (1974), and he struck a note of weary fatalism in *Buffalo Bill And The Indians* (1976) as Ned Buntline, the journalist who manufactured a Western legend. After enduring some late 70s disasters – *The Island Of Dr Moreau* (1977), in the old Charles Laughton part, *Go Tell The Spartans* (1978) and *Zulu Dawn* (1979) – he re-emerged in Spanish director Luis Buñuel's distinguished *Atlantic City* (1980) as a broken-down old numbers runner poignantly nursing fantasies of a gangster past.

with Shirley Booth in Come Back, Little Sheba

JANE RUSSELL

JANE RUSSELL

Real name **Ernestine Jane Geraldine Russell**
Born **Bemidji, Minnesota, 21 June 1921**

The second thing one notices about Jane Russell is her abundant good humour — the comfortable scepticism of a big luscious broad eyeing the antics going on all around her. Those antics began in 1940 when Howard Hughes chose the busty young chiropodist's assistant to star in *The Outlaw*. Early in the nine months of filming he decided that 'we're not getting enough production from Jane's breasts', whereupon the designer of monster aircraft like the 'Spruce Goose' repaired to his drawing board to dream up a brassiere specifically engineered for the task of enhancing Miss Russell's equally formidable cleavage. *The Outlaw*, an offbeat Western much of which was directed by Howard Hawks, opened briefly in San Francisco in 1943, and for the next seven years became the subject of extended legislation over its suitability to be granted a code seal of approval. At one point a Baltimore judge observed that Russell's breasts 'hung over the picture like a thunderstorm spread out over the landscape'. When the film finally went on release in the US in the early 50s, the poster showed Russell stretched out invitingly on a pile of straw, fondling a pistol while her blouse threatened to burst asunder, with the caption 'Mean, Moody and Magnificent'.

The movie made big breasts all the rage but, unlike Jayne Mansfield, Russell was not merely a top-heavy freak. Her acting ability was certainly limited (although she studied acting at no less than Max Reinhardt's Theatrical Workshop and with the formidable Maria Ouspenskaya), as was evident in *Young Widow* (1946), but with experience she matured into an amiably efficient professional: as a comedienne in *The Paleface* (1948) and *Son Of Paleface* (1952), trading wisecracks with Bob Hope and achieving the somewhat unlikely feat of producing a whole litter of children for him while she's in prison; as a drolly erotic mate for a comatose Robert Mitchum in *His Kind Of Woman* (1951) and *Macao* (1952); and as a good foil for an aging Gable in *The Tall Men* (1954). She could sing, too. She was one of the 'Two Little Girls From Little Rock' in Hawks' *Gentlemen Prefer Blondes* (1953), much more at ease than Monroe and memorably surrounded in a gymasium by serried ranks of compliant musclemen. In *The French Line* (1954) playing a cheerful, husband-hunting oil heiress, she warbled two startlingly direct songs while audiences admired her bosom in 3-D. She looked great in a bathing suit in *Underwater* (1955) but, ironically, that was the year in which Mansfield made her first spectacular appearance in a bikini. Russell's last film of note was *The Revolt Of Mamie Stover* (1956), in which she was a 'saloon girl' in Agnes Moorehead's bordello, singing 'Keep Your Eyes On The Hands' to the customers.

In 1957 she produced and starred in *The Fuzzy Pink Nightgown*, a satire on Hollywood with a great cast — Ralph Meeker, Adolphe Menjou and Una Merkel — but a great flop. Thereafter she slipped into a well-upholstered semi-retirement, punctuated by guest spots in the odd low-budgeter (*Fate Is The Hunter*, 1964, *Johnny Reno*, 1966, *Born Losers*, 1967) and a juicy role in an old-fashioned thriller, *Darker Than Amber* (1970). She has appeared on Broadway in Stephen Sondheim's hit musical 'Company' and on TV modelling bras for 'us full-figured girls'.

with Clark Gable in *The Tall Men*